Praise for FLIGHT RECORD

FLIGHT RECORD is an exquisitely written logbook of hidden truths, arrivals and departures, and lost distances. With warmth and meticulous. spare language, Bruce McIntosh invites us in to his personal inquiry, and through his heart-led quest, guides us toward a keener understanding of absence, of presence.

— SUSAN HAYDEN, author of
Now You Are a Missing Person

FLIGHT RECORD digs deep into the ambivalences of a father-son relation — closeness and distance, similarity and difference, love and hate. Through a keen sense of the intricate and endless details that make a life, Bruce McIntosh brilliantly spins the poetic kaleidoscope of his relation to his father from youth to age, naive connection to hard-won self-awareness.

— LEO BRAUDY, cultural historian and film critic,
author of *The Frenzy of Renown: Fame and Its History,*
The World in a Frame: What We See in Films

With razor sharp seeing and a wise, spacious heart, Bruce McIntosh takes us from his boyhood to the end of his father's life. As I read each finely chiseled gem of a poem, a mirror was held up to my own life, as a daughter who has struggled to come to peace with her mother. This is a stunning collection that illuminates the pain, love and tenderness that bind families together.

— DEBORA SEIDMAN, author of *The Lilac Minyan*

FLIGHT RECORD

FLIGHT RECORD

poems for my father
by
Bruce McIntosh

PINEHEAD PRESS

FLIGHT RECORD

Published in Santa Fe, NM

PINEHEAD PRESS

www.pineheadpress.com

ISBN: 979-8-9880528-1-4 (paperback)
ISBN: 979-8-9880528-2-1 (epub)
Library of Congress Control Number:
2025903679

Cover design © 2025 by Susan Emshwiller

Author photo by
Michelle McIntosh

To all fathers and sons

FLIGHT RECORD

Part One

1

My balloon from the church fair 1962
gets away from me by the two-car garage
off into the summer sky above the trees
Watching it shrink high above
I ask where it's going
I can't remember what you said
Where are you now?
in that sky, that same sky?

2

On the other side of that garage
by the weeds around the back door
side by side peeing
boy dick man dick
side by side
Instructions on the etiquette of outdoor pissing:
"Don't let your mother or Mrs. Wardell
Or any other woman see you do this."

3

And on indoor pissing:
(In the bathroom at the head of the stairs)
"You can either shake it
or use a few squares of this toilet paper
to dab it dry."
You shook yours so I shook mine
I like to think a few trees have been saved
because I wanted to be like you
and still want to be like you
Have always used and will continue to use
the first method

4

Asleep in the lower bunk bed set against the wall
eight or nine years old about
Across the room near the doorway
there was noise that woke me up
You walked into the wrong bedroom
in a sweatshirt and khakis, I think now
Probably with shoes still on
talking to yourself
Strong smell which I later came to know:
Whiskey
You lay down on the bed groaning
I pasted myself away from you to the wall
So drunk you'd taken a right at the top of the stairs
instead of the left to your own room
Think of it: 33 years old,
29-year-old wife across the hall
four sons in bunk beds
I don't remember if you got up before dawn
making your way to your proper place

in the full-sized bed with a low maple headboard

trees out the small window against the night sky

the sky where you worked

I'm a boy
sunlit corner near Grand Central Station,
standing with other pedestrians waiting for a light
For a moment I was lost
looking around and seeing only strangers
tasting panic
standing frozen
searching to my left
You who'd disappeared suddenly reappears
bemused, friendly curiosity on your face
having observed your son in this new situation,
studied his response
Relief is not the word
I don't know the word
You said something
I hope you took my hand
on the northeast corner
most likely Madison or "Lex"
in the sunlight with the ad execs and secretaries,
the blue-bloods and messengers
in their 1963 clothes

6

Your bedroom then:
a little maroon and gold colored steel TV,
RCA black and white set with maybe a 12 inch screen
sitting on a cheap metal stand with plastic wheels,
and behind, along the wall,
"his' n her's" low maple dressers
In your second drawer:
a Playboy magazine or two
hidden under the folded white t-shirts and briefs
Photos of beautiful young women with thick hair bands,
shortish sprayed hair flipped up like half a wave
above the lovely flow of neck into shoulder

'62 I'd say
In the kitchen
you stand leaning against
the steel copper colored electric stove
smoking a Lucky Strike
You wear a red turtleneck
your hair neatly combed
(Parted the same from 1939 to 1998
slightly swept back from the front of the widow's peak
to the right)
You're talking to Mom
You are 31 and it is fall
Turning to your left and taking a step towards the hallway
a torch of flame shoots up your back
Mom yells:
"Peter, you're on fire!"
With a single beautiful gesture you whip the shirt over
your head and it's off
A burner still on,
what's left of one of the new miracle fabrics
smoldering on the floor
Your broad, powerful back

white and unscathed in the low kitchen light

The fake brick-look sheet of vinyl flooring,

formica counter with the stainless-steel edge

You did what had to be done

flawlessly fast and smooth

8

I'm 10
You wore a thick navy-blue waist length wool shirt
8 inch "V" opening at the neck
eyelets strung with a rawhide lace
the "Ponderosa Shirt"
khakis, a watch cap, pale tan/orange
Georgia brand work boots
cream colored rubber sole
You were moonlighting
driveway snow plowing service
'55 gray Jeep with a red plow
Sometimes I was with you
cold, the heater weak
You work the two steel rods
each had a maroon colored knob
the size of a canned Queen Anne cherry
One for up/down,
the other for right/left
Playing them like the machine maestro you were
4-wheel low in 2nd gear
slamming that snow into a lovely convex packed bank
The vacuum controlled windshield wipers

hissing their song

thin blades always a little behind the rate

of the falling snowflakes

A few passes and you were done

Leave and onto the next one

The picture book, gently curved driveways flaring

to meet the neat six paneled garage doors

little carriage lamps on either side

just-so snow on the domes of the shrubbery

a slate walk to the front doors

usually enamel red or black

flakes whirling down

At the top of your invoice pad:

the black ink drawing of a Jeep

windshield up and top down

Then:

"Pete McIntosh, Capitol 7 - 0414"

Leave the bills in envelopes in the freezing mailboxes

Some wouldn't pay

Sometimes the sons of bitches

with the biggest houses and longest driveways

were last to pony up

The kid's hungry and cold
so were you,
you who'd be flying the next day

9

Maybe I'm seven
overhearing Mom on a tan rotary phone saying:
"...no he's dead-heading to Buffalo."
"Dead" is bad!
He's doing something dead??
Just airline crew talk:
Meaning a company pilot is on board as a passenger,
can't fly another leg himself, would exceed FAA's
allowed hours at the controls for that week,
so he catches a free ride home, that's all
No reason for my little gut to tighten up
But now
you really are doing something dead
(whatever that is)
we'll all find out

10

Like some speck, I remember standing by you
a star spattered sky when I was a boy on the front lawn
We looked up and talked about stars
I've forgotten the words
I like to think you held my hand,
but it is unlikely
I remember pats or scruffing
on top of my crew cut head,
but no hand holding

Bob Hoffman protein bars, Ovaltine in a jar,

powdered Tiger's Milk in a yellow box

in the cellar "playroom"

whitewashed cement block walls and linoleum floor,

set of weights out of York, Pennsylvania

On the wall a black and white poster of Dan Lurie

in a small bathing suit flexing on a beach

big arms/ shoulders/ chest atop a tiny waist

then explosion outwards into enormous thighs and calves

You on a cheap weight bench doing presses and curls

I and at least one other of your sons

sit cross-legged on the floor watching

I think you would have preferred to be alone

but gave in to some "father-li-ness"

You couldn't really kick us out —

on what grounds exactly?

So we watched you strain and sweat

against the Pennsylvania steel on the Connecticut floor

to have big arms,

to want bigger arms

to be a 33-year-old pilot with four sons and a wife

and want bigger arms

You the drinker and smoker
after those big arms
Why?

Your four boys in the back of a dump truck
parked in front of a diner
quiet street on a Saturday afternoon
(us in our old striped t-shirts and scuffed brown shoes)
We waited for some time
The beat up multicolored scraped steel of the dump body
hot to the touch in some spots
Were you flirting with a waitress,
drinking coffee in a thick restaurant cup,
a green stripe on its rim?
Listening to her smoking a Kool menthol
lit off a matchbook
advertising a home correspondence school?
Local and working class,
she might drop last consonants:
"Where ya comin' from, Wil-t-ehh?"
Did you grab a quick Salisbury steak,
mashed potatoes and canned peas?
Or were you quiet in a booth
keeping an eye on the truck
nursing a milkshake with your smoke?
Just needing a few minutes,

some kind of break from a man's concerns,
looking out across the street to the wire factory
an old brick building with dirty windows facing
a set of railroad tracks stuffed with weeds
The forest slowly moving in to take over

13

As a boy
I liked saying
"Make a muscle."
You would shove up the sleeve
of whatever you had on
and to my boy eyes
a huge cream-colored bicep would swell up
instantaneously big as a grapefruit
My little fingers would squeeze it
astounded at its size and density
The inside of a man's upper arm
one of his most protected and smooth places
the immense live power of that arm
fed by big faintly-visible blue veins
No more blood of you around now though

14

We'd stopped at a little stable in the dump truck
I'm ten maybe
Local horse show on
Maybe Mom there with some of her students
There was a lunch truck with a grill
You got yourself, me and another son burgers to go
A few miles down the road yours
(A cheeseburger you'd put up on the metal dash)
slid off, falling onto the dirty rubber mat
and gearshift boot
You YELLED at me for not catching it
It was a ride over to NY State and
I did not speak for a long time
I was too little to make any
left-handed quick catches of anything
My stomach full and my hamburger still some to go
and you had nothing to eat
After another long time you said something
"Forget about it, it's no big deal,"
something like that
But that fury unleashed could not be erased
Shortly before you got sick

you came to LA at my request
to sit in a room with me and a counselor
When I spoke of this memory you said:
"I remember that."

15

I see you in Breckenridge, Colorado
on your back being loaded up by the ski patrol
It is late afternoon 1965
you in some black windbreaker
and some of the first buckle boots, leather
We were not big skiers
but went a couple of times
(The family could ride free on airline passes)
You grinning and joking with the ski patrol boys
You ever the tough little son of a gun
who smiled through a busted leg
Sun going, cold coming down the slope

16

It is the day before Christmas Eve
Guys come around the theater looking for money
I get home to a message
from another guy looking for dough
I bring wood in for the fire
Your granddaughter is excited
in the way of a ten-year-old American
girl this time of year
You didn't care much for Christmases
One time you sat drunk on the floor by the fireplace
leaning against an armchair,
made us sit and attend as you read from
one of the Gospel accounts as we squirmed around
There is a photograph of you on a ladder
hanging an ornament
when you had a mustache like your father's for awhile
Hung over, telling us to go back to bed
when we knocked on your bedroom door too early one of
those Christmas mornings,
or waiting forever for you to come into the room
coffee in hand
so we could begin opening gifts

Something wrong about Christmas for you
leaking into ours
Scary around you then, the drinking
So keyed up, we were
excited to borderline hysteria and the music:
sometimes Ray Conniff Singers Christmas album,
sometimes an old LP of Handel's Messiah,
but our boyhood holiday magic soured by
some cloud in you
over you
around you
some formation the escaping from which
an aircraft was of no use

Part Two

17

I remember you one night in a sliding glass doorway
trying to give me a 20
"You need some money?"
I didn't take it
Ralph and I were parking cars Fridays
at an expensive restaurant
I had a little teenage cash in my pocket
could keep the motorcycle gassed up
enough for the burger fry milkshake
movie or YMCA dance admission
Guys a year older dying
in landing zones on hillsides in Asia
Me jacking off and restlessly riding
around on the two-laners
You punching your high end clock
Ray-Bans on, looking through a 727 windshield
"Fly the friendly skies"

18

I squat beside you on a driveway cut into the woods
It is a summer day
I'm 12
A guy at the gas station is selling a Harley Sportster
it's maybe a '62 or '3
I drink it in
You look at it
You don't buy it
It's a pump jockey's teenage machine
loud and fast with rotten brakes
and handlebars that shake at idle
I know because years later I had a '69
guys coming up to me at the gas pumps
with their memories
"Yeah my brother had one a these."
Arrive dirty faced in LA after the two-day ride
clutch cable hanging by a strand
I only had it because of you
trying to be you
Thank you for that desert wind

19

I have just snapped at my wife
looking for a replacement light bulb this fall evening
Your granddaughter has a bladder infection
and drinks cranberry juice on the couch
watching a subtitled movie with your daughter-in-law
The snapping blast of anger so like your own
so like that which I heard too many times
Proud that my episodes are rare
but chagrined they exist at all
I remember Mom in tears
at the opposite end of the various dining tables
feel a flash of irritation at the nostalgic WASP playwright
writing of "The Dining Room"
Leaving out as far as I remember
the drinking, yelling, cruel silences
food being pushed around
air thick and heavy with the sadness
the paralysis after some tirade
some unkind words blown across the table hurricane-like
heavy hearted disappointment and frustration
of the hungover airline pilot
who at the moment wishes for some other life

knowing there is nothing to be done
events and turns of years past have
led to this chair at this table this night
with this wife and these sons
the odd hours and early morning drives back
dropped through three different time zones in two days
of course exact a price
to do this some years in a row and drink in the midst of it
the moonlighting - excavating and snowplowing jobs
all grind something in a man
have eaten something in you
there is now pain in each breath for you at times like this
these cruel words ride outward
from some sparking acid regret and sorrow
the air above and around the heads of your family
altered and saddened
and you too must swim in it now

20

You were drunk

We were at what you called the friendly dining room table

("friendly" 'cause it was big and round, replacing the old

rectangular one with the 90 degree corners)

 Somehow you and I got into an arm wrestle

my biceps and forearms half the diameter of yours

but as soon as we started

I knew I could easily beat you

I pretended it was very hard

I can't remember if I let you win

or if I won with a big feigned struggle

but it was an eye opener of the first degree

Something I'd been living under

fell away in a monumental landslide sheet

I was stronger than you by a mile

barely an inch taller

but 17-year-old football player

teenage chi blowing through my body

you instantly irrevocably dethroned

It was not without sadness that I took on this knowing

Connecticut granite chunk of boyhood

fell into a deep gravel pit lake forever

If I was to this level of man strength
then I no longer warranted your protection

21

One time

you told me your favorite color was red

One time

you told me you were an "ass man"

One time

you told me you quit drinking

One time

you told me you had a "Summer of '44"

You and flying:
I see the books, the charts
the plastic navigation tool,
(circular dial set on a rectangle)
the Ray Bans, uniforms, flight manuals, log book
sad at being too young to fly in WWII,
washed out in jet training after two hours,
30 minutes in a T-33
your hearing not good enough for instrument flying using
low frequency navigation tone coming off the radio towers
No F-86 over Inchon skies for you
Five years logging hours at little airports before
that first airline job
right seat in a DC-3
a wife & two little sons
plus one in the oven

23

Liquor store the next town over a gold mine

at an intersection

commuters drove through to the Westport trains

catch those wool-suited skinny tied heavy drinkers,

the into Manhattan train crowd,

plus others heading north to Bridgeport or New Haven

The proprietor keeping his shelves well stocked

for all you guys

with your deep demand for Scotch

Vermouth and bourbon and vodka and gin

bottles of tonic water

jars of maraschino cherries

You'd come home with a Lowenbrau

 blue and yellow cardboard box

the top cut off:

One six-pack,

the rest for the whiskey and vodka bottles

that clinked when you got to the dirt road

A few Triscuits with supermarket cheddar

not too many

leave the volume in the stomach clear

for the screwdrivers and whiskey sours

drinking on fall afternoons when it was still legally
possible to smell perfume of burning leaf pile smoke
You'd get it going
that drunken warm gut place
the poisoned brain quietly buzzing
couple hours relief
like so many others in those towns at that time
guys with Nazi helmets or Japanese flags
in their hall closets and attics
Work drink sleep work drink sleep
Work drink sex sleep
Work drink sleep work drink sleep
Mow the lawn drink
Swim drink swim
Play tennis drink
Play golf drink
Go to a cocktail party drink
Drive drink sleep
Fly land drink
36 years pass
until "they ain't no mo'"
as you sometimes said

24

The cold booze hands around glasses and ice
taking you from yourself and your family
leaving you lying face down on carpets
couches car seats garage floors
Wake up
razors in your eyes
sour anger in your heart
go back for more
that impermanent buzz
fleeting transparent shoddy
euphoria of a temporarily poisoned brain
then harsh head-shaking
trembling slurred anger and self-loathing
lukewarm metal taste of cigarettes smoked
bar nuts chewed
neck sweat and summer morning sun the chaser

Finished out your run in the DC-10

Airline makes you 737 Captain

but won't let you stay with the fun short hop plane

Oh no, cross country for you

sometimes JFK to LAX non-stop

a stack of quarters on the throttles

crew bets on when and if they fall

six plus hours in the left seat

Try and get the co-pilot to do all

the announcements to the cabin

Liked skimming a few feet over a floor of clouds

at 600 mph hands and feet on the controls

Many guys would just do their leg on autopilot

you told me you flew yours

You wanted to know the plane

called some of the young guys "straight and level boys"

as long as the weather was calm and clear

and the aircraft systems behaved perfectly

they were great pilots

26

You had a '48 Indian Chief motorcycle
A guy on your block hated it
put a sugar cube in the gas tank
trying to wreck the engine
Each morning you would fish it out
Also a 61 cubic inch machine
you bought on time from Harley of Manhattan
got it paid off in the dead of winter
partway to Bedford Hills turned around and went back
They slid your frozen hands off the grips
You couldn't uncurl your fingers
Bought a windshield and they put it on
and you made it home
You told me about these bikes
and the way the father-son dance proceeds
I of course had to freeze my hands and face
on old Triumphs and Harleys when I was young
like you on your machines in 1947
when you also were briefly young

Wide feet size 7 triple "E"
bowling pin calves, average thighs
big back deep chest
thick deltoids, biceps, forearms, wrists, fingers
hairless torso and back
black-haired hands and arms and legs
numerous root canals and fillings
medium weight black beard shaved in the shower
green eyes
pilot eyes
One time in high school I come home
I call your name
I mean I never called your name
you were only "Dad"
not "Peter" or "Pete"
Looking for you I go into the not too big master bedroom
with cathedral ceiling
Now thinking of it I know these things:
The doors were all hollow core
nicely stained but cheap
Surprisingly there you were in the bathtub
The tub itself some low-slung thing

brushed steel framed

sliding shower stall doors open

There you are this little naked guy

"Come on in."

We talked of something as you got up to towel off

the big FORCE

the fierce HEAD OF THE PRIDE

With no clothes on looking small

another miraculously made scared human

same as me

28

Drunk
you'd taken the sidecar rig out at night in the snow
wearing your insulated red suit and black gauntlets
and run it off the dirt lane between rocks and trees
then staggered home in the cold
In the morning we helped you get it out
I don't remember now for sure
but think we needed a length of rope

29

One time you told me you wanted to write

I remember you on a stool

at the kitchen counter maybe 1966

I stood at the far end of the room

watching you read Bob Dylan's poetry off the back

of an early album cover

Sweatshirt on probably a cigarette possibly a beer

It was night

winter I think

the kitchen light not great

but you sat and read as I watched

I think you read all the poems

and when you finished

"Pretty good" you said

something like that

Did I know you too well?

my internal simpatico radar tuned too fine

could tell what was on your mind

heard the tires of those Fords on driveway

my stomach my whole system would go tight and alert

Wait to see:

Uniform jacket off?

Pilot hat pushed back off your forehead?

Two flight bags in hand?

Slow step fast step?

Drunk sober?

Hung over?

Quiet loud?

All of the above?

31

Calendar on kitchen wall next to refrigerator
In the days of week squares, at top, penciled in
with start/stop arrows:
"JFK - DEN - SFO"
"He's on a trip."
"He has a trip tomorrow."
"He gets back from a trip Tuesday."
"He bid an LA trip this month."
"He's not here, he's on a trip."
 Where have you gone off to this time?

Rotten sleeper lousy eater:
Wheaties instant coffee with
Cremora and 2-3 sugars
sometimes your wife's fried eggs hard on the edges
white toast margarine from a round plastic tub
Rinse the plate
leave in the sink for "later"
no favorite food I can think of
too many airline and hotel steak dinners
cheap ice cream
(More often after quitting drinking)
Milky Way or Three Musketeers
whole milk
Concentrated frozen orange juice
tap water with ice

33

One afternoon after school high school
April or May
You sit alone at the head of dining table
"Danish Contemporary" on thick yellow carpet
behind you sliding glass doors open onto the second
floor deck, beyond the thick woods
countless leaves flipping in sunlit breeze outside the
sliding glass door slid open to the wooden deck
You are barely intelligible
muscles of tongue and mouth try
to obey directives of alcohol drenched nerves
I present you with a mimeographed sheet -
word problems:
Trains leaving at different times
from different destinations,
if they both arrive at station X at 6:45 AM
what is the difference in speed
between train A and train B?
You study the sheet
limp mentally down the sentences
make a few slurred out loud notes of the particulars
start over from the beginning several times

then apologize and
give up
I say that's OK
and go downstairs
You the jet pilot
crocked into near oblivion on a weekday afternoon
alone in your house
The #1 son with black heartedness hands
schoolwork to you
pale violet text of so-so mimeograph
cuts you enough rope to hang yourself
then sick/sad, retreats
the drunken man
his sober boy
two different rooms two different floors
The sound of trees
hitting their respective ears

34

As a teenager
I grab a half gallon glass jar
Tropicana orange juice from the refrigerator
unscrew the metal top
take a big swallow
foul metal poisonous taste
WRONG BOTTLE
one big cold screwdriver

Much driving while drunk
standard at the time
Seat belts were optional equipment
Big V-8 auto trans American sleds
driven all times of day or night
Drunken executives, copywriters, and pilots
roaring down picturesque suburban roads
many times wives and or children riding along
I remember being driven back from swim team at the "Y"
from the next town over in a black Galaxie with other
teammates, you drunk and speeding
maybe we were 12
old enough to know that 70 was too fast
for night driving with children aboard
drum brakes and weak headlights
the two-laners without sidewalks or streetlights
little driveway notches between the stonewalls and trees
kids on bicycles
Cats dogs possum deer raccoons squirrels
all endangered by you men
Many veterans of WWII or Korea
AM radios playing Frank or Tony or Steve and Eydie

trying unsuccessfully to outrun suffering

in your big cars 60 miles out of Manhattan

Throats of the carburetors sucking air and cheap gasoline

Butterfly valves jammed open

connected by linkage to the feet of you men

riding the long rubber covered accelerator pedals

attempting to outrace your unbeatable fearsome pain

36

You would say:

We pass this way but once

Now, when there is more behind than ahead...

Hang in there

Paddle your own canoe

kicked out of the nest...

peace

As long as you're under my roof...

Eat what's put before you

There but for the grace of God...

When you're young, you live for yourself, then you live for your family

Don't do things for your family, do them for yourself

...keep the wolf away from the door

The world is your oyster

Tuck that shirt in

Put your knife and fork at twenty past four

Keep it down to a dull roar

Up and at 'em

Go outside and find something to do

Turn that boob tube off

Turn that idiot box off

That's not bad

not too shabby

This thing's cattywampus

It's right where you left it

You won't do that again

That'll learn ya, durn' ya'

Gol-dang

Jeezem crow

Jesus H. Christ

Jeez Louise

Lookout, Louise

Get your butt in gear

Apply some elbow grease

Keep your eyes on the horizon

Always look around, check if your wings are level

That hit the spot

He's got a hollow leg

burning a hole in your pocket

son of a sea cook

goombah

Their taste is in their mouth

He's full a crap

He's hard on machinery

Standby one

Negative

He's got a severe case of "headus implantus rectumus"

Watch it now

out there in the land of the lotus eaters

trolling for queers

son of a gun

son of a bitch

screw it

Keep it down

Quiet!

Miss "Got-rocks"

That's enough of that noise

Let's "malletize" this

We're going to have to "Americanize" this bolt head

Let's persuade this

Dress this with this file here

Grease this

Oil this

Lubricate this

Adjust this

a touch

A little here

little this way

to me

to you

good enough for government work

that bastard

Get on the end of this

When I tell you, do "x"

all right, sports fans

all right, Tiger

Bruce der goose

That showed lack of judgment

That's what I like to see

Pause in between the gears like this

I'm going to show you boys how to use tools and it's going

to save you time and money

your mother and I

Hold the fort

Hang tight

I don't want you to worry

When you're old enough, I'll tell you a joke about King

Farouk on a bar stool

accident of birth

in those days

Keep the revs up

Don't lug it

Check with your mother

You're all set

squared away

the cousins

the tea company

lad

37

Frozen waffles Log Cabin syrup

margarine Quaker Instant Oatmeal packs

brown sugar/cinnamon

get as much sugar into a high school kid's body as possible

to start the day

common practice then

You lay on living room carpet between couch

and coffee table passed out

as your wife and kids do their morning thing

no good

Me feeling shaky walking out the sliding

glass kitchen door

across the deck to the motorcycle for

the short ride to school

sunlit trees

their thousand leaves stirring

38

Sir, I think of you once again
white t-shirt with a blue crew neck and
YMCA logo over the heart
You went down there to play handball
took me once and the pang of the little ball
(I was terrible)
then to the new locker room
into a sauna for the first time
cold shower after
Now I wonder
was this what you'd do for a hangover sometimes?

39

I see you

from the back

sitting up straight

in a Lee Rider jean jacket

on a tree lined road

I'd finished a trumpet lesson

driving the high school music teacher nuts

with my no talent no practice regimen

and afterwards the Jeep wouldn't start

one of your dead mother's horse farm Jeeps

You came over on your motorcycle

black '66 BMW R50

maybe it took you five minutes to get that Jeep going

I followed you

down that straightaway with

the lovely trees and stonewalls

little ragged grassy shoulders meeting the pavement

you ahead sitting up tall

the quiet sound of the German motor exhaust

What if all time exists at once

and you are still on that road behind the low windshield of

the black fairing

summer air velvet

in fourth gear gliding home

your son behind you?

40

After that first airline hijacking to Cuba
you and some of the other pilots put
pistols in your flight bags
The FAA could go "f" itself
yours was a .38
(They didn't X-ray the pilots' bags back then)
9/11 the United jet over Pennsylvania
What if one of the flight crew had picked up this habit
from you, was up front that morning
could he have somehow got to his firearm?
Son #2 told me that late in your career
you still were "packing"
He asked: "Isn't that illegal?"
Your reply: "Nobody's taking my plane."

41

Back from Salt Lake trip
You'd seen a Black man on a street with one shoe
Told him, "I've got enough for both of us today."
In the shoe store he picked out a pair of white slip-ons
You said, "You're sure thats's what you want."
(thinking lace-up, six-eyelet, thick-soled oxfords like those
in your closet would be better)
He stuck with the white ones and you paid

42

Pilot "walk around" of the rented Cessna
"See, I'm checking this."
Working a cable to the flaps and rudder
making sure everything was behaving properly
When we landed you tried to teach me
how to taxi back with the rudder pedals
I couldn't get it
doing these rough "s's"
after a few minutes of letting me try
you took over
instantly as if on rails
you run that plane straight

43

August
humid dusk
back in the driveway from NY
after the flight back from Denver or Portland
Tick-tick sound
of the V-8 motor cooling down
Smell of summer trees
hot brake linings and coolant
motor oil and gasoline and you:
I don't remember now for sure, but always the after shave
Old Spice or Brut or Aqua Velva
best if you'd come straight home
no whiskey or vodka bouquet
better for all concerned

44

"Sometimes a paycheck is enough."
old school little diner one afternoon
blue collar gray sky winter Connecticut town
Bare spooky trees ringing the beat-up parking lot
Another time you told me
when mom and you were first married,
before work at the little airport outside Boston,
you and your 21-year-old wife
would stop at a diner
have oatmeal and coffee together at 35 cents apiece
How those were good times
because you struggled together
that without a long haul "victory" would not be so sweet
But 20 years later
drunk, you walk around inside your house alone
So this is what kind of triumph exactly?

45

Sometimes walking through rooms
you muttered
one sided conversations
sotto-voce telling-offs
of who knows who
eyes on the carpet
head gesticulating
pogo-ing on the neck
We could not make out the words
but the sound was there
Who were you talking to?
An out of control America?
Was it the farm boys in the rice paddies lost for good?
Or your ghosts -
your crippled father
your crazy mother?
Walking barefoot in your quiet house
maples and oaks and birches
out the windows listening to their own sound

46

From the back seat of the various Fords
en route to wherever
besides whiskey, sometimes driving your only peace
trips to your mother-in-law's outside Boston
Those days
where you lay on an air mattress in her pool
on your back
the Ray Bans shielding your eyes from summer sun
There is a photograph:
Pool water calm
you rigged up with some other inflatable pool toys
arranged such that you were supported behind head,
knees and ankles
alone, floating on top of the water
You were not a good relaxer
From the back seat of the Fords
looking across at an angle towards a 3/4 view of your face
and back of your head
the muscle of the clenched jaw before and below the ear
rippling the rear molars
clamping and unclamping for hours
What hellhound on your trail,

In your guts?
These kids this wife this job this life?
The pilot on the ground
behind the big wheels
of the broad-hooded cars
so rarely happy
I hope you found peace that afternoon in that pool

47

The early planes were not fancy
25 passenger DC-3's
heaters no good
windshields leaked
Bakelite plastic headphones made your ears sore
lousy static-y sound
roaring prop engines
metal skinned vibrating beasts
muscle them around on landings and take off
Heavy applications of "elbow grease"
to the yoke and rudder pedals required
to get safely on and off the runways
Come in on final approaches
in snow over Buffalo or Pittsburgh or Dayton
for flight pay
to chip away at the note on the little house
buy groceries and gasoline and school clothes
fuel oil for the winter
Long gone now
all of you guys and your planes

48

Summer 1950
Randolph Field
San Antonio, Texas
You'd ridden by train from Penn Station
after standing outside
your mother's closed door to say goodbye
said she'd never speak to you again
In the barracks a Frenchman
smokes Gauloise cigarettes
Laying on the bunk your first night
you wonder what you have done
21 years old
The first ride:
AT-6 Texan
"T-6"
tail dragger with one big radial engine and sliding canopy
in front of you a stick
simple round black-faced gauges
to your left a steel throttle lever
a steel trim wheel
On the floor two steel rudder pedals
these and the stick to the instructor's controls

sitting behind you in his own cockpit
Taxi out and up into the summer sky
He throws the plane around in stalls
spins rolls until you vomit
After landing and shutting it down
he tells you to clean up your puke

49

In the small master bathroom with its shower stall:
Small bottle of Vitalis for the hair
steel can of Noxzema shaving cream
steel "safety" razor with a machined handle
Twist grip at the bottom would
open these little steel doors to accept the rectangular
double-edged blades
"Safety razor"
Tried one once
felt like the blade was trying to tear the skin off my face
You guys tough back then

"Whiskey tenor"
(as you classified your singing voice)
near perfect pitch
Come home drunk:
The Limeliters: Live in Concert
The Clancy Brothers with Tommy Makem
Crank it up loud on that lousy living room player
sip from the Galliano bottle
(an odd one, 2 and a half feet tall
like an upturned table leg)
gold colored sweet liqueur on your aching throat
living room lights up full
windowpanes filled black with night
You singing lonesomely loud

1966
 I'd saved up for my first stereo
bottom of the line Sony "HP-150"
little turntable with two speakers
but nice stained wood
brushed metal with a "smoked" plastic dust cover
You'd taken took me over to the next town
Roger, a college kid you knew was on the floor
You rode him hard:
"It's a 'demo', Rog.
What can you do on that price?
This looks like a scratch here."
When we got home it was early evening
I set it up in the room I shared with a kid brother
Mom came in and at least two of the sons
It was getting dark,
but I still had the lights off and we listened:
"Hello, darkness my old friend..."
All were admiring of this sleek new thing in the house
Were you there?
(Though musically gifted
you had this crappy old Sears stereo

down in the living room

awful looking, with rotten sound

fake black grain covers and brown grill cloth

on the speakers)

You, a poor negotiator on your own behalf

("I buy dear and sell cheap.")

who'd gone to bat for me and saved some precious dollars

lovely music in my room

but none in yours

52

Maybe 1965
The guy from the dry cleaners with the Elvis hair a few
steps into the kitchen
dropping off the box of cleaned and pressed airline shirts
uniform pants on hangers with the cardboard insert
thin clear plastic covers, matching suit jacket,
holding them all,
talking about "...the niggers down in Norwalk..."
cotton shirts with the epaulets
wool/cotton blend plain front pants
narrow lapel suit jacket, smoky blue
two or three navy stripes near the sleeve's end
(Years later a Black man we knew
driving a dump truck, picked me up hitchhiking:
"Your father knows how to treat poor people...
Told him I was looking into being a carpenter
Next time I see him he hands me
a starter set of brand-new tools.")

53

I was 19

in the afternoon

Lee Rider jean jacket and the hood up on the TR-4

leaning over the driver's side fender doing something

surely something you'd taught me

You came out and stopped beside me, to my left

my hands in the engine

Suddenly your right hand

the palm of your right hand was on my back

a little below my shoulder blades

You let it rest there

the warmth of it

the light pressure

the only time I remember you touching me like that

Young strong bands of muscle on either side of my spine

moving slightly as I worked

You'd quit drinking for some six months plus

quit in your own tough/weak way

the same method used with your Kool Menthols:

Stop cold turkey after 22 years of whiskey and vodka

I like to think that at that moment

in that driveway you loved me

broke the Yankee WASP hard cast airline pilot strictures

to touch your grown son's back
this laying on of a hand

54

One time in Beverly Hills at a restaurant
(you flew the next morning)
We sat around a dim lit place, maybe Chinese
There were drinks with umbrellas and you had one
I thought: This is no good:
First, it's a violation of FAA rules
your departure time too close for you to be drinking
second, I hated to see you drink at all
because of thousand times
I'd seen it come to no good effect
You looked tired
and your face had thickened up in a lonesome way
When a pilot knows work is "x" hours off
something in him is readying for it
has a hold of him already
I was sad to see you break the rules
Don't you understand?
Sons want their fathers perfect

55

Another time I visited on a gray morning
The hotel in Beverly Hills
a little south of the "world class shopping district"
half a block north of Pico
on the outskirts really
I had a '64 Mercury I'd bought for 275 dollars
out in the Valley one night
Had a 390
beige and the headliner hung down
One time the accelerator linkage jammed open when I
floored it pulling out on PCH
and the brakes -
It needed drums all around
I wanted you to see it
We ended up taking a little ride on the side streets
You drove
nailed the gas pedal
tore past the low houses with tile roofs
and immaculate lawns
I was crossing my fingers
hoping the linkage wouldn't hang up again
But writing this now

why should I have been worried?

You the pilot

would have followed an emergency procedure

calmly put the shift lever in neutral

kill the ignition glide to a stop

Then if there was time

baby it down Pico to a hardware store

Buy some WD-40 and carb cleaner

make the linkage right, knowing you

you couldn't make life right

You couldn't make your wife or son's lives bend around

but you could make sure the vehicles were just so

that could be accomplished

If a man gives some of his time to that

it could be love

to free up linkage

don't you think?

Part Three

56

There are four sons
You called me last
"A little challenge" you called it
"ALS" aka "Lou Gehrig's Disease"
You were 62
I did not trust your words
Drove to a good bookstore
In the medical reference section:
INCURABLE
kills in 1-3 years
Called the other sons to share these facts
They wept
(one didn't)
not sure who
We all did graveside

57

Summer
loose fitting swim "trunks"
on lower-rent stretch of south Malibu sand
I see your atrophied shoulder
your disappearance underway
I stand next to you
We look out across the surf to the west
maybe shin deep in the water
You tell me your last physical
your eyes test 20/20 and 20/10
Those 63-year-old eyes so lovely and green and sharp
now of course human eye dust
Are there little flecks of green somewhere in your buried
ashes, like mica?
Glinting like a moonlit snow-covered lawn?

58

29 Palms

Same summer you were diagnosed

August

The idea was that the men

that is, you and your 4 sons

would go somewhere together

We rendezvous in Los Angeles

Drive to the desert

older motel complex with a pool and restaurant

Next morning after breakfast

we stroll over

to the horseshoe pit

start playing

old sand, weathered boards

big iron horseshoes

First the sons go as I remember

then you take a shoe in your right hand

hold it up shoulder height

aim at the rusted post

at the far end of the pit

Taking your bead

sighting through the "U" of that horseshoe

you bring it back and make your toss
It falls with its sound into the sand
its old iron sound into old sand
Makes it 2/3 the length of the pit
five feet shy of the post with its dead sound
Now we cannot get around it
The four sons who threw easily to the post or past
Now we know your right arm
the strength of it and your shoulder is being sucked out
to go back where it came from
The disease is vanishing you
going to whisk you before our eyes
off the sandy cheekbone of the planet
You are going to be shaved off
thrown to the sky never to return
There is no getting around the short throw
your best throw
Five feet shy
You are dead, motherfucker
We've all seen it now

59

You hurt your throat laying on a bed watching TV
in some hotel room in some city on some trip years before
Eating a roast beef sandwich
It gets caught in your windpipe
a long coughing fit scarred your throat
After you were sick but could still walk
I sat next to you in a second run movie theater in L.A.
a lot of trouble clearing your throat, "ahem-ing" away
I asked if I could I get you a soda
You said "No."
too tough

60

On sidewalk Vermont Avenue south of Los Feliz
My car parked across the street
A break in traffic we start to jog across
"I don't run so good." you say
Your arms and legs jerking
Like a marionette worked by
some unskilled puppeteer
You who took nylon shorts and running shoes
on your pilot trips a few years before
now this
your last run

61

One spring afternoon
when you could still walk
we went to a little airport on a windblown ridge
Your airline pilot friend had flown
recon planes in Vietnam
owned a surplus one and had asked for pictures of it
(I took them for you - your weakened arms, hands,
shoulders and legs precluded climbing onto wings and
getting photos of the cockpit through the canopy needed)
You directed me from the ground
until we had the required shots
I came down to the grass
and we headed for your car
You walked slowly
with a pronounced tottering limp
Your motor nerve fibers disintegrating
You who loved motors so
your own now seizing and smoking and burning
leaving you to rock unsteadily in knee-high grasses
past the end of the single runway
sun starting down

I drove you to a Manhattan hospital
Your hands and fingers and starting to go
clinical trial for an experimental drug
a narrow little room with a guy and his stopwatch
You faced a counter
wearing one of your brown leather pilot's jackets
twisting a little to your left in the chair
Timed "dexterity test" :
Your right hand to pick up quarter inch little steel dowels
from a plastic cup then distribute them into a tray
with Oreo sized depressions
trying to get your hand and forearm to work
When you finish
the guy checks his stopwatch and clipboard and says:
"Last time you were faster."

63

A fast jump to that hospital bed in the dining room
Construction paper on the wall towards the ceiling
Christian Science therapist
positive thinking magic marker sayings:
"I am not my disease, etc..."
Daughter-in-law's few up there too,
Buddhist prayers beginning with
"May you be..."
Good wishes notwithstanding
you are dying, Jack
Suck of the ventilator blowing air
into a rig cut into your neck
Another hole below the rib cage on the left side with a
plastic fitting accepts the end of a rubber feeding tube
where they pour in the milkshake
Dump it straight into the stomach
like you and me with a piece of garden hose
siphoning gas from a jeep gas tank into a can
to fuel another of your vehicles
for another of your many endless projects
all of which will now remain undone
Lay in that bed

Watch TV

Sleep

Observe your arms, thighs, and calves shrinking

no more projects

64

When you sleep the eyelids don't always close
The nurse tells me that can happen
the night nurse, the 11 PM to 7 AM angel
who massages Lubriderm into your toes and soles
She takes them one at a time from the open-faced boots
with velcro straps that hold your heels down so your calf
muscles don't shorten and bow your insteps over and
curl your toes into the balls of your feet
Your jaw muscles frozen
larynx and voice box control gone
baby grunts on the exhale
then lungs inflated by the machine to the left of your bed
dry air blown down your throat
You're on the "vent"
as the nurses say

65

A nurse has to change the sheets
I help roll you onto your right side
I push and brace your back
your testicles visible
red/violet against white atrophied thighs
those balls from whence I came

67

A year and a half into ALS
in a wheelchair in the kitchen on a December morning
you look out the bay window at the sons running two
backhoes in the cold to dig you a trench
from the new barn to cross the driveway
You're pissed:
"He better go get that load of gravel because if it freezes,
the job can't be finished until spring.
He better take the Goddamn truck and get over there."
It's only that you can't run a backhoe
You can't go outside
freeze your dying ass off with your sons
Never again will you drive operate ride or fly machinery
Electric wheelchairs don't count

68

Christmas
the dining table with extra leaves set up in the living room
family seated around it
You at the head in a wheelchair
lost in a tan cardigan cashmere sweater of your dad's
shrunken
trimmed silvery beard
the lovely once powerful slightly freckled shoulders
deflated to bone
their bands and curves of muscle vanished into the sky
to see your shoulders gone
the sweater as if on a hanger in a closet
the "living" room

69

A November Sunday morning

I drop the receiver

hands up fast to clasp top of my head

walk around the living room

"My dad died."

In the bedroom

my wife and six-year-old daughter lay on either side

tears rivers what new literary way to put it

Father dies

Son cries

You enter the world

from between your mother's legs

your own to atrophy

and be incinerated

emptied into an urn

placed on a bolt of tartan

which we carefully lowered

into the grave cut into the gently sloping hillside

our knees pressed into the frozen grass

We stand to shovel the dirt back in

On the ridge the guy on the bagpipes

walks slowly back and forth

Four pairs of legs
(Your sons' legs)
balance on feet and shoe leather awhile
and finally move away
to the gravel lot and car interiors
to then stand around on the living room carpet
The universe gave you two legs to use
In turn you provide eight legs to continue on:
One set in offices
another laying against English saddles
another underneath engines and drive shafts
the last on various stage and film set floors
Your own lain slack for some years on sheets
on the hospital bed facing the bay window
not moving unless a nurse shifted them

70

In my closet this morning

I take out your old navy-blue wool watch cap

from the top bureau drawer

also an average watch with steel band

gold colored with black face

not a rich man's watch

I slide it on my once in awhile

A leather pilot's jacket you gave me

the lining starting to pull away at the collar

A plaid polyester western shirt you bought too small

In the hall closet the London Fog raincoat

from when the airline uniforms were dark blue

I occasionally wear it for a few minutes

put it on to get some kind of hit

of you who are so dead

I smell Yuban coffee and Domino sugar

whiskey and old struck out hotel matchbooks

Kool menthols and Dial soap

In the pockets

sometimes little airline logo plastic stir sticks

crumpled foil from a stick of Dentyne

maybe a couple dimes

I hear you

An auditory hallucination because I miss your voice?

In dreams you'd show up once in a while

the months after you died

Now I can't remember your last appearance

Is that a border?

When you quit showing up in a son's dreams?

The real "gone-ness" of gone?

72

A slice that is you
This guy you find outside
in a driveway at dinnertime
bent over a motorcycle
wrench in hand
an old pair of coveralls
yours
your very clothing on

73

I think of your friends:
Dave, "flat top" haircut, gut, one leg shorter than another
low work-oxfords
one with a big thick remedial sole
pointing to the side when he walked
Master mechanic who had a Shell station
He didn't visit much when you were sick
I didn't see him at the funeral service
Tony, United pilot, older, lived two towns east
Italian-American, bomber pilot in WWII
came home and married the widow of a shot down friend
quit coming early on
did not see him at the service either
(His wife was there, but then women are stronger)
A couple of other United guys did attend
did keep coming to see you
The thing I don't want to say is that
you lived without close friends
and so died without close friends

74

In a cardboard box in storage was a pair of
black low boots with an ankle strap and a square toe
You wore them flying
the still polished boots of you
the middle-aged airline pilot
Driving his 240Z or BMW 2002 to Kennedy or La Guardia
Park, walk over to the crew bus
(looked like a school bus shortened by half
painted navy blue, the United color)
Go up to the flight office and sign in
Check on the weather printouts
Sip paper cup coffee "light 'n' sweet"
Walk outside onto the winter pavement below the jetway
J-2 fuel smell hanging in cold air
Go up the steel steps
Sit in the right seat after hanging up your uniform jacket
Look over preflight checklist
A "stew" pokes her head in
"You guys want anything?"
(Maybe hung over a little
when you got up for the 3AM shower and shave)
Did it turn into just a job?

Grind of time changes and airline meals
hotel rooms and now and then a rough captain
Annual flight surgeon physical
two FAA check rides a year
flight school for new model aircraft
Four East Coast teenage sons doing who knows what
as you drop down on afternoon final approach in Denver
or Salt Lake or Portland or LA
a Kool menthol with breakfast next morning
Get ready to do it all again eastbound
Home after the hour and a half drive out of New York
Arrive mid-afternoon to an empty house
stuff laying around the kitchen
always the fresh stream of bills
three and a half days off
How could you be dead?
You who kept mom and my brothers and me alive
with your labor all those years

75

Lovely eyes

towards the end your only means of expression

Your mouth and jaw frozen up pretty bad

You couldn't really smile

A yawn working its way through somewhat

but your mouth couldn't open

muscle fibers atrophied and shortened up

only the green eyes

long lashes

no, I'm making that up

I don't know if they were long

but the eyes

I believe I could draw their shape and angle of their set

and get it right

They're air now

I don't know if green dead eyes

burned in an incinerator leave ash

or go up in smoke

how that works

but they're gone

I am here
you are not here
Your Jockey t-shirted and briefed body has been
reclaimed after its loan to Capital and United Airlines
and "family unit"
Your withheld federal taxes being partially
pitiably small-ly mailed to your widow once a month
your headstone a quarter mile away
Big trees down a bank
border the cemetery lawn

77

The Zen master asks me:
"Where is he now?"
 Me:
"I don't know."

Thanks to:

Susan Hayden

Susan Emshwiller and Chris Coulson at Pinehead Press

David, Veronica, Michelle, Antoinette, Dawn, and to all those who were there early mornings on Sugar Lane back in the day